D0786264

JUL 2 6 2012

Leopard & Silkie

One Boy's Quest to Save the Seal Pups

Brenda Peterson • photographs by Robin Lindsey

Christy Ottaviano Books

Henry Holt and Company • New York

It's sunrise when Leopard is born on the shores of the chilly Salish Sea. He is a golden, spotted seal pup. But he still has a thick and wavy white newborn coat. Leopard weighs a little more than a bowling ball and is shorter than a skate-board. On this late summer day, Leopard gazes out at the big world around him.

First, Leopard nuzzles with his mother.
And then he drinks a bellyful of rich milk.

As Leopard nurses, his mother memorizes
her pup's scent and sounds, so she can find
him when they are apart.

Now Leopard is ready to explore the beach.

He uses his foreflippers to hop and slide along the sand.

When Leopard's mother encourages him into the surf for his first swimming lesson, Leopard is only one hour old! Leopard makes a call just like this: *"Maaaaaa!"*

Some days, Leopard plays in shallow rock
pools. When he gets tired, Leopard climbs
atop his mother's back to catch a ride.

Leopard is a little older. Onshore, his dry fur shines lighter and he's grown plump. His mother tucks him in a secret cove to rest while she fishes nearby. She will come back and nurse her pup. Leopard often naps for eight hours while his mother is gone.

Is Leopard safe onshore?

There are helpful adults and children like Miles who make sure pups are protected.

Every day during the summer, Miles looks for pups on the beach. He is a kid volunteer for the organization Seal Sitters. Miles knows it's natural for pups to nap onshore because they are unable to swim for long periods of time.

One morning, Leopard is alone onshore waiting
for his mother. But when the sun comes out, so do
all the people!

Soon the beach is filled with two-legged giants.

They bark in strange, high voices.

They come too close and chatter real loud.

"Is the seal dead?" children ask. "Where is the mother?"

The crowd is so much bigger than Leopard.

A skateboarder cruises by, a baby cries, a dog off-leash chases a Frisbee. It whirls like a flying saucer and lands right next to Leopard. *Thwack!*

Leopard is very scared. He has never seen people before.
Will they hurt him?

Will they steal him from the beach while his mother is offshore?

If the beach is crowded with onlookers, sometimes the mother
may be too frightened to return to her pup.

Leopard shivers and covers his face to hide
from all the bustle.
    But the noisy people come closer and a boy
tries to touch his flipper.

"Please!" says Miles. He's on beach patrol with his dog, Lulu. Miles always keeps his dog on a leash. Dogs can bite, and Leopard is too little to protect himself. "This pup is just resting. The mother may be watching us from the water," Miles explains to the crowd.

Then he asks everybody to stand back and put their dogs on leashes. Everyone listens.

By noon, the crowds grow bigger. Miles uses his mother's
cell phone to call other Seal Sitters. He helps string caution
tape around Leopard that reads "Protected Marine Mammal."
The tape is like a big, yellow crib on the beach to keep the
curious people a safe distance away.

Like other kids, Miles loves to watch Leopard with his binoculars. Leopard stretches up and arches his body to cool down. Then he trustingly rolls on his back and yawns.

Leopard is relaxed enough to sleep.

Miles wonders if Leopard's mother will return with so many people on the beach. Loud trucks rumble by and wake Leopard.

I've got an idea! Miles thinks. He quickly leaves with his grandfather.

Back at their home, they spend several hours building a large platform of plywood and foam. A floating island for the pups! This way, the pups won't have to come ashore when the beach is crowded with people.

Later that afternoon, Miles and the other Seal Sitters row out into the cold waves.

Together, they tie the raft to a buoy just offshore.

Will Leopard leave the land and swim out to wait for his mother?

No, Leopard remains on the beach. Is he too
scared to swim out to the raft by himself?
Miles and the Seal Sitters wait.
Where is Leopard's mother?

At sunset, a glossy head rises in the waves.
Leopard's mother scans the beach for her pup.
"Maaaaa!" Leopard cries out, and very quickly
he flop-hops from the beach into the surf.

Then Leopard and his mother do something exciting—
they leap up onto the raft Miles built.

At twilight, the seals wave and flap their flippers.
Another young seal and even a cormorant, a web-footed
waterbird, join them.

The Seal Sitters go home very happy.

Days come and go. Miles and the Seal Sitters watch Leopard and his mother swim together. Leopard learns how to catch fish. And every sunset, they rest on the raft. But one evening, when Leopard is five weeks old, his mother does not return.

"Why doesn't the mother come back?" Miles asks his grandmother.

"Leopard is being weaned," Grandmother explains. "He must fish for himself. But it's not easy at first. We've really got to keep our eyes on Leopard now!"

Miles and the other Seal Sitters worry about Leopard. But they cannot feed him. Leopard will have to survive on his own. He belongs in the sea.

After several weeks, Leopard is too thin. His skin is loose. His stomach sags. Catching fish for himself is hard work!

One sunset, another seal pup scoots onshore near Leopard. Here is Silkie. She is older, her fur is whiter, and she's more plump.

The two pups shoot up through the waves, mouths wide open. A big bite—and Leopard catches many fish in his tiny new teeth. Before long, Leopard is healthy again.

Silkie is like a big sister to Leopard. Diving down together, Silkie shows Leopard how to hide and even nap in kelp forests. Scientists say that seals dream, just like humans do.

Now every day, Leopard and Silkie slip onshore together.
Kid Seal Sitters rush home from school to go to the beach.
They do their homework while they keep watch over the pups.

Leopard and Silkie have found a safe shore they can share with human friends.

Most of all, they've found each other.

As for Miles, he dreams of the pups swimming together nearby in the Salish Sea.

Author's Note

When beachcombers report a baby seal on our Salish Sea shores in Seattle, Washington, neighborhood volunteers rearrange their busy lives to sit in shifts, forming a quiet and protective circle around the seal pup. We call this Seal Sitting, or babysitting seal pups while they rest and nap onshore. Scientists call this caretaking of another species besides our own "allomothering." All animals, including humans, do it. It's like interspecies adoption.

Every late July through September in Puget Sound (or the Salish Sea), mother seals give birth onshore, sometimes in rookeries or nurseries, other times alone on the beach. For hours each day and night, adult and infant seals will rest onshore. Here they can nurse, regulate their body temperature, and seek community with one another. It is an important time in their busy lives.

There are fewer and fewer natural beaches left where seals can find sanctuary. That's why when a pup is resting and warming his body on the beach, it is important to make sure dogs are kept on leashes as we walk the beaches. Dogs and seals can carry diseases that cross species and harm both kinds of pups. Under the Marine Mammal Protection Act, it is recommended that people stay one hundred yards away from seals. Harassing a marine mammal is a crime. Also, if the mother returns from fishing and finds her pup overwhelmed with people, she may abandon him. A nursing pup separated from his mother rarely survives.

But people are curious—and concerned. Often they do not realize that it's perfectly natural for a pup to be napping alone on a beach. Seal Sitters will surround the pup with caution tape. We've been trained by the National Oceanic and Atmospheric Administration (NOAA) to talk with passersby and educate them about how lucky we are to be sharing our shores with wild animals. And if we protect them, the seals trust us. They even sleep deeply. Scientists have shown that seals actually do dream; they experience REM sleep, just like humans. Sometimes seals drift in kelp forests and sleep with their heads just above water, bobbing about in the "bottle position."

Though Washington State has a healthy harbor seal population, only 50 percent of newborns survive their first year. Climate change and warming, more acidic oceans, pollution, and overfishing are reducing the number of fish that seals depend upon for food. Wild predators, dogs, infection, dehydration, starvation, ingestion of plastics from balloons or bags, and human interference are also real threats.

NOT ON OUR WATCH! Sitting with seal pups teaches us that we are not alone on this fragile blue planet. We are among friends. Please visit Seal Sitters at sealsitters.org.

To all the seals who grace our shores and to the volunteer Seal Sitters
and members of the Northwest Marine Mammal Stranding
Network who help keep our beaches wild and safe for sea life

Special thanks to Miles, his parents, Elana and Yuri, and his grandparents Sergey and Diana.

And much gratitude to our Seal Sitters core team: Nancy Leimbacher, Jane Martin, Candace Sullivan, Leo Shaw, Toni Frohoff, and Larry Carpenter. We are also very grateful to the City of Seattle for its neighborhood grant to increase public awareness and education on seal conservation. And to the Parks Department for its wonderful alliance in protecting marine life on our shores.

We are fortunate to be guided and continually educated by our NOAA Marine Mammal Stranding Specialist, Kristin Wilkinson, and our astute Washington Department of Fish and Wildlife marine mammal research biologist, Dyanna Lambourn. We thank PAWS Wildlife Center and Wolf Hollow Wildlife Rehabilitation Center for their dedication to saving seal pups and other wild animals.

Our children's book agent, Erin Murphy, was the first to believe in this project, and she found the perfect editor, Christy Ottaviano, who nurtured and inspired us every step along the way. Seal pups on every shore find true allies in Erin and Christy.

This book is for Brenda's beloved brother, Dana Mark, and her sister-in-law, Renee. And to her parents, Max and Jan, who first taught Brenda to love wildlife. To our next generations—to dolphin researcher Courtney; to Charlotte and Alex, who volunteered as Seal Sitters on their honeymoon, and to their new son, Liam; to Christina, who first introduced Brenda to her chameleon; and to Katy, whose kindness also embraces other animals. We so appreciate Tracey and Lulu, neighborhood volunteers. Also many thanks to all our kid Seal Sitters, including Etienne, Noemi, and Anasophia; and to their parents, especially Janet, Carolyn, and Mishele.

Robin dedicates this book to her family, most especially to her mom and dad for their love and support. And to Joanie, Blue, and Mary, who try their best to understand her seal obsession, for their treasured friendship. To Kristin for her generosity and abundant patience. To Dyanna for sharing her rookery world and for being a true and passionate mentor. To Toni and Brenda for their ceaseless dedication to making this a better world, and for their guidance and friendship. But most of all, to seal pup Leopard and all the little Silkies who truly saved me—you who taught me not to be afraid to go below the surface.

Bibliography

Courtney, Jeni, Eileen Colgan, Mick Lally. *The Secret of Roan Inish*. VHS. Directed by John Sayles. Culver City, CA: Sony Pictures, 1994.

Hewett, Joan. *A Harbor Seal Pup Grows Up*. Minneapolis: Carolrhoda Books, Inc., 2001.

Hodgkins, Fran. *The Orphan Seal*. Camden, ME: Down East Books, 2000.

Martin, Rafe, and David Shannon. *The Boy Who Lived with the Seals*. New York: Puffin, 1993.

McKnight, Diane. *The Lost Seal*. Oxon: Moonlight Publishing, LLC, 2006.

Morris, Jackie. *The Seal Children*. London: Frances Lincoln Children's Books, 2004.

Henry Holt and Company, LLC
Publishers since 1866
175 Fifth Avenue, New York, New York 10010 [mackids.com]

Henry Holt® is a registered trademark of Henry Holt and Company, LLC.
Text copyright © 2012 by Brenda Peterson
Photographs copyright © 2012 by Robin Lindsey,
except image of pug © iStockphoto.com/falcatraz
All rights reserved.

Library of Congress Cataloging-in-Publication Data
Peterson, Brenda.
Leopard & Silkie : one boy's quest to save the seal pups / by Brenda Peterson ; photographs by Robin Lindsey. — 1st ed.
p. cm.
Includes bibliographical references.
ISBN 978-0-8050-9167-0 (hardback)
1. Seals (Animals)—Conservation—Juvenile literature. 2. Wildlife rescue—Juvenile literature. I. Title. II. Title: Leopard and Silkie.
QL737.P63P38 2012   599.79—dc23   2011029041

First Edition—2012
Printed in China by South China Printing Company Ltd., Dongguan City, Guangdong Province

10 9 8 7 6 5 4 3 2 1